FUN
with
NUMBERS

A+
books

Can You Guess What ESTIMATION IS?

by Thomas K. and Heather Adamson

Consultant:
Tamara Olson, Associate Professor
Department of Mathematical Sciences
Michigan Technological University

CAPSTONE PRESS
a capstone imprint

A+ Books are published by Capstone Press,
1710 Roe Crest Drive, North Mankato, Minnesota 56003.
www.capstonepub.com

Books published by Capstone Press are manufactured with paper
containing at least 10 percent post-consumer waste.

Library of Congress Cataloging-in-Publication Data
Adamson, Thomas K., 1970–
  Can you guess what estimation is? / by Thomas K. and Heather Adamson.
     p. cm. — (A+ Books. Fun With Numbers)
  Summary: "Uses simple text and photographs to describe estimating"—Provided by
publisher.
  ISBN 978-1-4296-7557-4 (library binding)
  ISBN 978-1-4296-7858-2 (paperback)
  1. Estimation theory I. Adamson, Heather, 1974– II. Title. III. Series.

  QA276.8.A33 2012
  519.5'44—dc23   2011021342

Credits

Kristen Mohn, editor; Gene Bentdahl, designer; Svetlana Zhurkin, media researcher; Laura Manthe,
     production specialist; Sarah Schuette, Photo Stylist; Marcy Morin, Studio Scheduler

Photo Credits

All photos by Capstone Studio/Karon Dubke

Note to Parents, Teachers, and Librarians

This Fun with Numbers book uses photos of everyday objects in a nonfiction format to introduce
the concept of estimating, including estimating number of objects, estimating measurements
such as length with nonstandard units, and estimating time. *Can You Guess What Estimation Is?*
is designed to be read aloud to a pre-reader or to be read independently by an early reader. The
book encourages further learning by including the following sections: Table of Contents, Taking It
Further, Read More, and Internet Sites. Early readers may need assistance using these features.

Printed in the United States of America in North Mankato, Minnesota.
102011   006405CGS12

TABLE of CONTENTS

What Is Estimation?

How many fish could there be in this tank?
They're hard to count because they keep moving!
You can estimate when you don't need an exact
number. An estimate is a careful guess.

How many? How long? How far? How much?
These are just some of the questions you
can answer with estimates.

Estimating How Many

To estimate the number of fish, start by estimating one part of the fish tank. Count quickly!

There are about 10 fish in the box. Maybe there are a few more or maybe a few less. But 10 is a good estimate.

About four boxes this size fit in the tank. Add 10 + 10 + 10 + 10. That's about 40 fish in the tank!

Estimates can help you compare sets.

Emma's twin cousins are having a birthday. She wants to give each cousin about the same number of balloons.

Which two bunches of balloons are about the same?

Yum! Candy! Here is a pile
of 10 candies.

10

100

Here are 100.

?

How many are in this pile? Compare the piles. The
amount is between 10 and 100. Let's estimate to
get close to the real number.

Look at the pile of 10. About six of these groups of 10 would fit in the mystery pile.

Skip count by 10 six times to estimate the total. That makes about 60 candies in this pile.

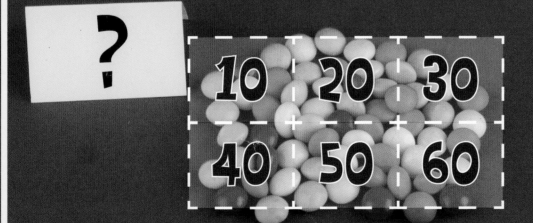

Now check your estimate by counting the candies. How close was it?

Estimating How Many More

Now try beads. Which pile has more? Are there more red beads than blue beads? Which pile has the fewest?

Jamie is making a bracelet. Estimate how many more beads he will need to finish the bracelet. Look at how much string is left. About how many beads will fit in that space?

Estimating comes in handy when cutting out cookies. Using the heart cookie cutter, you can cut five cookies in one row.

The star shape is bigger. About how many star cookies can you make in this row? More or less than the hearts?

Which of these cookie cutters will make the most cookies?

Are There Enough?

Who's hungry? All 15 children on the field trip want an apple. About how many apples are in this box?

Count how many are in the first row. Then skip count the number of rows.

Will there be
enough for everyone?

17

Estimating Length and Height

Choo choo! Becky's train can't get to the station without more track. About how many more of these tracks does she need?

Mom says not to fill up with ice cream. But how many cones would equal Luke's height?

He is about eight ice cream cones tall!

An ice cream pail is taller than a cone. Will we use more pails or more cones to measure Luke? Guess how many pails it will take.

Estimating Time

You can estimate how long something takes. Estimate how long it will take an ice cube to melt on a hot day.

Will it take minutes or hours?

Try estimating something shorter.
Jack just started blowing a bubble.

Will it take minutes or seconds for the bubble to pop?

23

You can estimate whether something will take more or less time.

Eric made an obstacle course. It took him 10 seconds to crawl through the tunnel, walk across the board, and hop the hoops.

He adds a cone maze at the end. Do you think it will take Eric more or less than 10 seconds this time?

Estimating for Fun!

There are lots of reasons to estimate. Sometimes we do it just for fun! If you make the closest guess to the number of jelly beans in the jar, you win the jelly beans!

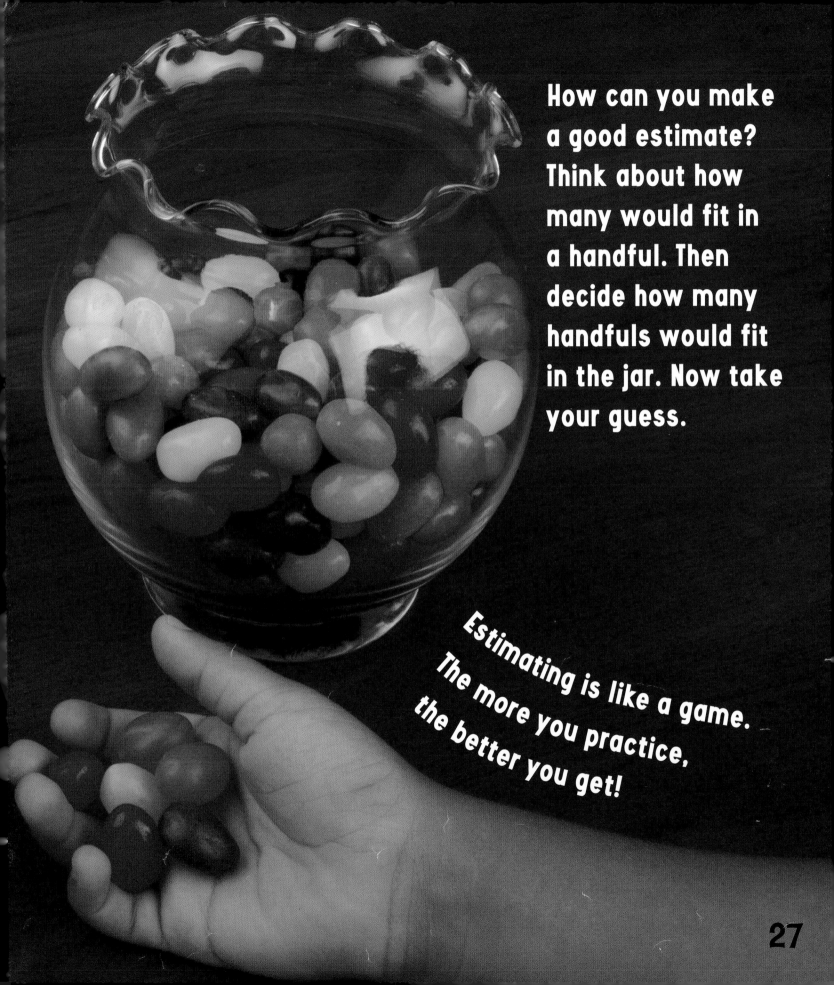

How can you make a good estimate? Think about how many would fit in a handful. Then decide how many handfuls would fit in the jar. Now take your guess.

Estimating is like a game. The more you practice, the better you get!

27

REASONS TO ESTIMATE

when things are moving

when you don't have a
measuring stick

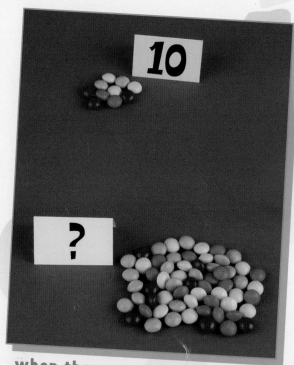

10

?

when there are too many items
to count quickly

when you're trying to plan ahead

when you can't see all the items to count

HOW CLOSE WERE YOUR ESTIMATES?

Pages 8-9:
The first and third bunches of balloons are close to the same amount.

Pages 18-19:
It will take about three more pieces of track to get Becky's train to the station.

Pages 10-11:
There were 62 candies in the mystery pile. Our estimate of 60 was pretty close!

Pages 20-21:
It will take fewer ice cream pails than ice cream cones to reach Luke's height. Luke is about four pails tall.

Pages 12-13:
Jamie will need about seven or eight more beads to finish his bracelet.

Pages 22-23:
On a hot day, the sun would probably melt an ice cube in minutes. Bubbles usually pop in just seconds!

Pages 14-15:
You could make about two more star cookies in that row—four all together. The smallest cutter would make the most cookies.

Pages 24-25:
It would take Eric a little more time to run the course after the cones were added.

Pages 16-17:
If you skip count 5 four times, you get 20 apples. That's more than enough for 15 children.

Pages 26-27:
The jar has about 130 jelly beans in it. How close did you get?

Look at the beads on page 12 of this book. If the red pile has 50 beads, about how many beads do you estimate are in the green pile?

How many students are in your class? Now use that number to estimate how many students are in your grade. If you have about 20 children in your class, and there are three classrooms in your grade, that would be 20+20+20=60 children in your grade.

Next time you're at the grocery store, estimate how long it will take you to wait in line. If one person takes about 2 minutes to check out, and there are three people ahead of you, how long will you wait? 2+2+2=6 minutes! You can practice estimating other things while you wait.

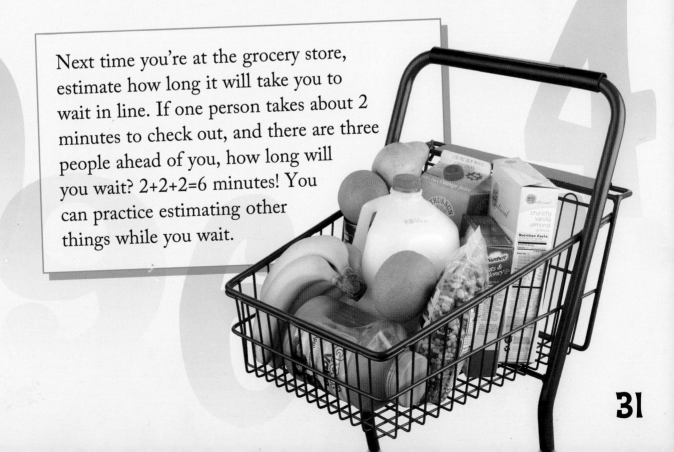

READ MORE

Dalton, Julie. *Farmer's Market Rounding.* Rookie Read-About Math. New York: Children's Press, 2007.

Dowdy, Penny. *Estimation.* My Path to Math. New York: Crabtree Pub., 2008.

Goldstone, Bruce. *Greater Estimations.* New York: Henry Holt and Co., 2008.

INTERNET SITES

FactHound offers a safe, fun way to find Internet sites related to this book. All of the sites on FactHound have been researched by our staff.

Here's all you do:

Visit www.facthound.com

Type in this code: 9781429675574

Check out projects, games and lots more at
www.capstonekids.com